Portree

ORIGINS AND EARLY HISTORY

Ella Liley

The Islands Book Trust

Published in 2015 by the Islands Book Trust

www.theislandsbooktrust.com

ISBN: 978-1-907443-29-9

Islands Book Trust
Laxay Hall
Laxay
Isle of Lewis
Eilean Siar
HS2 9PJ
Tel: 01851 830316

Typeset by Erica Schwarz (www.schwarz-editorial.co.uk)
Cover design by Raspberry Creative Type
Printed and bound by Martins the Printers, Berwick upon Tweed

Contents

Preface

The fact that Portree might have a history, or even at one time not have existed at all, had never occurred to me – at least, not until we had to pick a subject for our final assignment in the first of the series of Local Studies courses run by Aberdeen University. Everyone seemed to have a pet subject to research – except me.

Our tutor, in exasperation, selected a few of the old maps we had been working on, pushed them across the table to me and said, "Find out more about these!"

'These' were photocopies of the 1903 Ordnance Survey map of Portree and district. That exercise was really just a case of fitting the buildings of the village into chronological order, but later, during another Local Studies course, I found the old maps of Portree and was fascinated.

This is the result. It is not a definitive history. If anyone would like to add to or alter any of the following I would be delighted to hear from them.

CHAPTER 1

In the Beginning

It became quite popular during the eighteenth century for the adventurous to mount an expedition (for that surely was what it would have amounted to) to explore the Highlands and Islands of Scotland. The literature of the day, which emphasised the wild scenery and the 'noble savages' (the natives) encouraged exploration. The building of roads, like General Wade's, to open up the Highlands made travel marginally easier.

In 1773 James Boswell and Dr Samuel Johnson, travelling round the Highlands of Scotland, were among Portree's first tourists. They dined at the inn in Portree on their way from Raasay to Kingsburgh, retracing the route taken by Charles Edward Stewart – Bonnie Prince Charlie. Boswell then wrote about their journey in the much quoted if not so well read *Journal of a Tour to the Hebrides.*

There was very little anyone could say about Portree at the time, as the village was not yet in existence. There was only a scattered population round a sheltered bay, a church, an inn and a corn mill. However Boswell was not to be stuck. He explained that Portree, in Gaelic *Port Righ*, meant King's Port or Haven, and had acquired its name after King James V called here during his tour round the Hebrides in 1540. He does not say where he got his information, though it may have come from Sir James MacDonald, 16th Chief and 8th Baronet, and his brother Alexander whom he knew in London and Edinburgh. Both brothers were brought up and educated in England, so while Sir James is reputed to have communicated with his servant in Gaelic when they were in Rome, perhaps his Gaelic was bit rusty. Boswell certainly never asked the locals.

'Port Righ' or even 'Portrigh' instead of Portree, does not appear on any of the old maps, not even on Stobie's MacDonald estate map of 1766, where it is spelt 'Portrie' – Portrie Parish, Harbour of Portrie etc. All the other place names on that map are Gaelic, so if Portree really meant King's Port, why was it not written as 'Portrigh'? Why, in a Gaelic speaking area, would the name have been 'anglicised' from Portrigh to Portree, in the two hundred years since the king's visit? While on Martin Martin's map of the Western Isles from *A description of the Western Islands of Scotland*, 1703, Portree is completely ignored, on Timothy Pont's map of 1654, Portree and the bay are shown as 'Portray' and 'Loch Portray', which, if it were written phonetically does not sound very much like *righ* – king.

The 'Portray' spelling seems to have been in general use in the mid-17th century. The Sleat sennachie (story-teller, historian, record keeper and genealogist), Hugh MacDonald, lists the lands belonging to 'Sir James MacDonald of Slait and Donald, his eldest son'. These lands included 'Portray'. Then there is a record that 'MacNicol of Portray' was one of sixteen members of the Council of the Lord of the Isles which met at Finlaggan on Islay. The final meeting of this council was held in 1493 – half a century before James V's visit.

W. J. Watson, in *Celtic Place Names of Scotland*, gives an alternative translation, confirmed by many Gaelic speakers:

> Portree in Skye is often pronounced in Gaelic *Port-righ*, as if in 'King's port', and the name is supposed to date from a visit of James V in 1540. The unsophisticated Gaelic pronunciation of Skyemen, however, is *Port-righeadh*, and the second part is clearly from *righ* or *ruigh*, 'fore arm', common in our place-names as 'slope' or 'ground sloping up to a hill'.

So Portree should be translated as the 'Port on the Slope'.

One of the first authors to repeat Boswell's translation was the Rev. Alexander Campbell who compiled the Old Statistical Account for Portree only twenty years later. He seems unhappy about it and suggests the king in question might be Alexander III, who sailed up the west coast after the Battle of Largs in 1263.

Boswell also stated in his *Tour of the Hebrides* that Sir James MacDonald had intended to build a village at Portree and again, we presume he got his information from Sir James himself. Now, Sir James had been an exceptionally clever young man and when he died in 1766, eight years before Boswell and Johnson's visit, he was mourned as a sad loss to the island. But, while the estate map of Portree drawn in 1766 has a rather fanciful town superimposed on it – much grander than the twenty-two houses he had mentioned to John Mackenzie of Delvine, the MacDonald's Edinburgh agent – he hadn't built the village. So, why even mention it? Boswell may well have had his own axe to grind. He (one among many) had wanted to marry his distant cousin Elizabeth Bosville. When she refused him, Boswell, to save face, had let it be known that it was because she did not want to live in Scotland. So when she married Alexander, the first Lord MacDonald (Sir James' brother) and went to live on Skye, at least part of the time, poor Boswell felt very hard done by – and perhaps a bit foolish!

Elizabeth's rejection of Boswell in favour of Alexander made him hostile towards his former friends, the MacDonalds and he let it show in his writing. He complained of the sparseness and poverty of the accommodation the MacDonalds provided for them at Sleat. In his book, Boswell said that the MacDonalds were on their way to Edinburgh and had borrowed the factor's house at Armadale to accommodate them. They had actually come back from Edinburgh expressly to entertain them. Boswell suggested that Alexander was being miserly and had, "come from his seat in the middle of the Island (Monkstat) to a small house on the shore, as we believe, that he might with less reproach entertain us meanly". Then Johnson insisted that a Clan Chief should keep his clansmen around him and dress his servants better than himself, as he would do, were he a chief.

Johnson, it seems, could not resist telling other people how to run their lives – like a maiden aunt expounding on how to bring up children! Later in their tour when they visited the MacLeods at Dunvegan Castle, Johnson insisted that they 'should not leave the Rock' when Lady MacLeod said she wanted a garden. The strange thing is that the MacLeods had employed a gardener at the Castle for decades.

When the book was first published Alexander objected strongly to being depicted as a miserly host and an unsympathetic clan chief. When he protested indignantly, threatening violence, the more offensive passages were cut out and others credited to Dr Johnson.

So, was this mention of Sir James' village just another chance to make Alexander appear inadequate as a clan chief, by showing how the estate might have benefited if the older and cleverer brother had lived?

While Boswell's derivation of Portree is noted in the OSA, Alexander Campbell does not mention Sir James' desire for a village. However, he does give Sir James the credit for building the school and as schoolmaster, he reports on the subjects taught and how many pupils are ready for university. He then describes the bay and surrounding country and says it is an ideal spot to build a village, but does not even suggest any plans for development.

Boswell's two statements about Portree have been repeated so often, in almost every book written about the place, and now on the Internet, that they have been accepted as the truth. And we have all the road signs on the island to prove it – and, since the upgrading of the square, on the very stylish signs at the bus stop.

On his Grand Tour of Europe, Sir James MacDonald was accompanied by Adam Smith, the Scottish economist who wrote *The Wealth of Nations* and who was then Professor of Moral Philosophy at Glasgow University. He advocated building villages as a means of bringing industry to the Highlands. Sir James had probably absorbed Smith's ideas on villages, but died before he could put any plans into practice on Skye. He had died in Rome in 1766 where he had gone to recuperate after a shooting accident while hunting in North Uist. This accident, apparently, led to the invention of the trigger guard.

Portree did not come into existence until fifty years later so he could hardly be said to have founded the village, as some authors have expressed it. Nor did his brother Alexander, who inherited the chieftainship and baronetcy, and eventually became the first Lord MacDonald. With his brother, he was brought up in England and was educated at Eton and St Andrews. Boswell called him, though not Sir James, the 'English-bred Chieftain'. He married Elizabeth Bosville of Thorpe Hall in Yorkshire and took very little interest in his estates in Skye. It is his son Alexander, the second Lord MacDonald, who could claim to have founded Portree.

Only a year after the death of his father in 1795, Alexander, the second Lord MacDonald, was making plans to build a village at the 'Harbour of Portree' – not at 'Kiltaraglen'. Kiltaraglen has always been thought of as the ancient name for Portree before it was, supposedly, renamed in honour of the King's visit. One name did not immediately replace the other. Both existed side by side until the expansion of the village reduced Kiltaraglen to the area round Kiltaraglen Cottage. On the 1877 Ordnance Survey map, 'Kiltaraglen' is written in large letters across the Home Farm fields.

The name Kiltaraglen may be derived from Talorgan or Talorcan, the Culdee monk who is said to have built a chapel there. Kiltarlity, near Inverness, has a similar derivation. Culdee comes from 'Celi De', meaning Clients of God. They were a fraternity of monks who belonged to an ascetic revival movement which originated in eighth century Ireland as a reaction to the increasing secularising of the church. According to Alexander Nicolson in *The History of Skye* both the Bile and Kiltaraglen were Culdee sites. Jonathon MacDonald translates Kiltaraglen as 'the chapel at the foot of the glen'.

Before being built over by the village, there were thirteen tenants living in Kiltaraglen. They all paid a similar rent to Angus MacDonald, who:

> ... for his possessions of Kiltaraglen, pays to Sir Alexander MacDonald, or his factor, 15 merks of silver ... six pecks of meal, an eighth of a stone of butter, three-quarter parts of a wedder, a hen and a half, and a peck and a half of horse corn.

These rents, paid in kind, gradually changed to cash as a 1608 precursor to the Statutes of Iona required landowners to levy regular rents on their estates to pay Crown taxes.

As he had outlined to John Stanhope, Lord MacDonald had planned to create a better fishing village at Portree than the British Fisheries Society had done at Stein, in Waternish.

CHAPTER 2

Fishing Villages

At this time building villages was seen to be the answer to all the problems in the Highlands. Adam Smith, along with David Hume and John Knox, Scottish economists and philosophers, thought that this would bring industry and so employment to the Highlands. According to Smith, 'the town was a continual market where country people exchanged their raw materials for manufactured goods'.

Anything that kept their tenants at home was fine with Highland landlords who relied on their rent-payers and kelp-workers to raise sufficient money to keep them in the luxury to which they had become accustomed. Since Culloden and the arrival of the first sheep, the rate of emigration and consequent loss of income was a cause for concern. The Government, worried about the loss of army and navy recruits, wanted the Highlanders to stay at home. It was not till the advent of the Crimean war that the government realised how many of the Highland army recruits had been lost because of emigration.

Apart from Stornoway, which was already a thriving fishing town, there were very few settlements of any size on the west coast in the latter half of the 18th century. The Duke of Argyll had designed and built Inveraray and encouraged the development of Oban. Plockton, on the other hand, had a slightly different origin. It was developed from a straggle of cottages into a modern village by Sir Hugh Innes in the early 1800s to give homes to the victims of his own clearances.

The British Fisheries Society also wanted to develop villages in the Highlands to persuade Highlanders to take up fishing instead of rearing their black cattle. Even if they owned their own fishing boats, Scottish fishermen were losing out to the Dutch government-backed fishermen. They lacked piers or slipways, gutting and curing facilities, access to salt for curing – salt duties being very restrictive – and access to markets. So the British Fisheries Society, with the backing of the Government who saw fishing boats as a training ground for Navy recruits, went in search of suitable sites for their proposed villages. John Knox, in his *Tour of the Highlands and Hebrides 1768*, lists 'Loch Brackadale, Lochbay, Portree and Elen Oransay' among the 'Stations for Villages in the Hebride Isles'.

In 1788 the Society decided to start with just two villages at Tobermory and Ullapool. Ullapool did become a fairly successful fishing village, while Tobermory, with a good harbour, a newly built customhouse and the Caledonian Canal under construction to the north, depended more on trade than fishing.

The Society had chosen the site for their next fishing village but had not intended to start work there immediately. Lochbay, in Waternish, was thought to be ideal – but so, according to the OSA, was Portree but it had not been considered. Perhaps the ground here was too similar to Tobermory where the village had to be built on two levels – another 'Port on a Slope'. Lochbay on the other hand had plenty of flat or gently sloping arable ground and many families waiting to emigrate who would change their minds if given the chance to fish or farm there. Negotiations to buy the land from MacLeod began in 1789 and took much longer than expected. Thomas Telford designed the village in 1790 but construction difficulties were numerous. By the time an inn, a school, a storehouse and a pier were built at Stein four years later, the prospective tenants had emigrated. Their replacements found that, while the quantity of farm land provided was the same as at Ullapool, the quality was so much better that it made fishing unnecessary.

Colonel Alexander MacLean of Coll had warned the Society before embarking on their project that '...if the inhabitants can procure the bare necessities of life by their labour from the grounds they possess, their ambition leads them to no further effort'.

It was all due to mismanagement, Alexander, the 2nd Lord MacDonald, told John Stanhope when he visited Skye in 1806. Alexander had spent almost as little time in Skye as his father had, but took more interest in his tenants and did not like to see them, 'wandering the world'. He had his own ideas of how the local fishing industry should be managed. The fishermen should be provided with less ground than at Lochbay so that they were forced to go fishing. They should be provided with boats to be paid off by instalments so that, again, they had to go fishing to earn the money.

In 1804 he looked into the possibility of persuading fishermen from Peterhead, North Uist or Shetland to settle in Portree to help the local fishermen. As he explained to John Stanhope, he intended to bring in a fishing crew from Peterhead to help train the Skye crews: 'six men and having built six boats, to put one of these men in each boat with the compliment of Skye men. If they succeed, others will be glad enough to follow their example'. But in Portree the warning of Col. Alexander MacLean of Coll was justified, as the census of 1841 lists twenty agricultural labourers and only three fishermen and two coopers, though eight were listed as mariners or seamen.

In *The Islands of Western Scotland* W. H. Murray writes, 'MacDonald of Skye spent much money building fishing boats and engaging east-coast fishermen to train the Skyemen, but his efforts were wasted ... fishing never appealed to Inner Islesmen or Highlanders.'

CHAPTER 3

Portree as a Fishing Village

In his *View of the British Empire and Scotland*, John Knox provides a list of buildings required in any fishing village:

A key or breast for small craft

A range of warehouses for storage

Sheds for gutting etc and overnight accommodation

A small market place

A corn mill

A church and house for the minister

A schoolhouse

A public inn

And dwelling houses for fishermen and tradesmen

At the beginning of the 19th century, pre-development, Portree was already being used as a fishing port, even without the first three on Knox's list. The rest were already there. John Stanhope, on his visit in 1806, describes the fishing boats in Portree Bay lowering their pennants on the arrival of their Chief. Portree, he said, would soon arrive at the dignity of a town.

To conform to Knox's idea of a fishing village, Lord MacDonald had only to provide the pier and fish curing facilities. Portree already had a market, inn, church, school and corn mill.

The Market

The Portree market, for the trade of sheep, cattle and horses was probably not the kind envisaged by Knox, though it did sometimes include cheese, butter and wool. It had been in existence since about 1580 when a licence for a twice yearly fair was obtained from the crown. The trade in black cattle began in about 1650. They were shipped from the Outer Isles, landed at Dunvegan or Uig and along with the cattle from the North of Skye, were driven overland to Portree. Portree was a popular market for those selling their cattle as there was sufficient grazing in the vicinity of the market stance for the cattle to recover from their journey and so fetch a good price. The local farmers, who had to put up with this invasion, were not so enthusiastic – though they did get their ground fertilized for free!

The Inn

The inn, the last item on Knox's list, was perched above the harbour, expecting most of its guests to come by sea, as the condition of the roads then was bad to non-existent. By the Statutes of Iona in 1609, landlords were obliged to establish inns to accommodate travellers. This was James VI's attempt to control the Highland chiefs and open up the Highlands to encourage an early form of tourism. In 1746 Prince Charles

Edward Stewart must have been thankful that his great-great-great-grandfather had such foresight when he dined at MacNab's Inn on his way back to France. Because of this event the inn (or the hotel on the same site) is, of course, known as the Royal Hotel.

The inn was very busy during the cattle markets in Portree, with buyers, sellers and drovers all looking for accommodation. As part of his village development, Lord MacDonald aimed to improve the roads to encourage more cattle dealers to come to Skye, and to improve the inns and stables to accommodate them. According to the 1850 map there were stables between Portree Hotel and the (Bayfield) Lane.

At the beginning of the 19th century the inn, like the rest of the village, was beginning to grow and a new inn was built alongside the old one. The Innkeeper was John Livingstone who had married Margaret MacDonald. They had two children. The MacDonald Papers of 1803 show the 'process of removing at the instance of Lord MacDonald, John Livingstone, tenant and possessor of Colishader and the Change House at Portree'. Lord MacDonald apparently did not succeed, as Livingstone was still innkeeper when their second child was born in 1805.

The Corn Mill

In 1810 the ground between the 'not-yet-built' Wentworth Street and the Crachaig River was divided between the Innkeeper and the Miller. The corn mill is one of the oldest buildings in the village – John Buy of Kiltaraglen was the miller in 1733. It appears on the 1766 Estate Map beside the proposed village plans. It became almost derelict by 1795 and was rebuilt, only to be destroyed by fire ten years later. It was repaired again in 1806 and a laid was constructed from the dam to the mill. It was still in use as a corn mill in 1914 when the children in *A Family in Skye* picnicked near it. Since then it has been a sawmill, a joiner's workshop and, it has also been suggested, it may at some point have been a wool mill, but with one at the other side of the village seems unlikely. It has recently been converted into residential flats.

The School

The school was established in Portree by Sir James MacDonald before his death in 1766, after the 'Committee for Managing the Royal Bounty for the Improvement of the Highlands and Islands granted £25 per annum to a schoolmaster and catechist in this barony'. Later the poor schoolmaster lost £5 of his salary to make up that of a missionary in Kilmuir.

The school was built on what became the schoolmaster's land at (present day) Kiltaraglen. There was also a Gaelic school sited beside the original parish church, about where the Medical Centre is now, but it did not appear on the 1810 map as it would have had a thatched roof and only slated roofed buildings were marked, and certainly none of the original black houses are shown.

Two of the early schoolmasters (about 1782), Edmund MacQueen and Donald Martin, are only briefly mentioned in the MacDonald Papers. It seems that the payment of their salaries was sufficiently noteworthy!

The best known schoolmaster, the Rev. Alexander Campbell, was born in 1770, the son of the tacksman of Corlarach near

Dunvegan. He graduated in Arts from Aberdeen University and was appointed schoolmaster and catechist at Portree by the Commission of the Royal Bounty in 1791. That same year he was commissioned to compile the 'Statistical Account' for Portree. At Luskintyre, on Harris in 1803 he married Margaret MacLeod, daughter of Dr. William MacLeod of Glendale and they had four children. The oldest, Isabel, was born in 1805 and then there were John, William and Alexandrina. As well as writing poetry, he collected traditional poems, which were published in *Reliquae Celticae* and *Leabhar na Feinne.* He became minister of the Parish of Portree in 1799.

During his eight years as schoolmaster Alexander Campbell frequently wrote to Lord MacDonald informing him of the need for a new school at Portree and one was eventually built in 1815 on 'The Street', as shown in the 1830 proposed street map of Portree, now Wentworth Street.

Murdo MacDonald, though not Alexander Campbell's immediate successor and, since the introduction of the Gaelic and Glasgow Society schools, not the only teacher in the village, is the only one listed in the Parish records and the 1841 and 1851 Census. He came from Lochcarron in 1828 with his wife, Ann MacKenzie from Kirkton. They had four children; Margaret born in 1830, John in 1833, Donald in 1836 and another younger child. He was a leading figure in public affairs in Portree for sixty years, serving as schoolmaster until the demise of the old Parochial School system on the coming of the Education Act of 1872, and subsequently as Inspector of Poor and as Registrar. His school was in several different locations during his time as teacher, but latterly on Wentworth Street, in what is now the Caledonian Hotel building.

In 1875 a new school was opened on the present site. It incorporated a house for the headmaster and a tower, all picked out with red sandstone. It was enlarged in 1911, sadly demolished in 1969 (bits of it lie under the Bayfield car park) and replaced by an ugly concrete structure. This one, in its turn, was demolished in 2008 to be replaced by the present school.

The Church

When the parish boundaries were redrawn in 1726, the Parish of Portree, stretching from the head of Loch Snizort to the mouth of Loch Sligachan, including Raasay, was separated from the Parish of Snizort. In 1730 a slate-roofed church was built above the 'Harbour of Portree', probably as the most central site. A walled burial ground was added twenty years later. Before that, it is said, the burial ground for Portree was at the Bile, below Torvaig, where there are the remains of an old chapel and small graveyard. It is a difficult place to reach by land or sea and most impractical for funerals. When Sir Alexander MacDonald died in 1748, his widow had a tomb built at Kilmore in Sleat from stone quarried at the Bile. An old burial site was discovered at Kiltaraglen near the site of the old Culdean church.

There was a Glebe attached to the church – the Chamberlain's House was built on the glebe, as was the most of the new village – but there was no manse. The first minister of the parish, Hugh MacDonald, did not need a manse as he possessed a two-penny land at Drumuie and one penny of Penadown and paid a similar rent to Angus MacDonald of Kiltaraglen. He was the son of Hugh MacDonald of Glenmore and was a graduate in Arts at Aberdeen University. He married his cousin Elizabeth, both being grandchildren of Sir James MacDonald, the second baronet of Sleat. His son, John and grandson Ronald emigrated to North Carolina on the *Balliol.* He was succeeded, after his death in 1756 at the age of fifty-seven, by the Rev. John Nicolson who was 'of the famous tacksman of Scorrybreck'. He did not live at Scorrybreck but at the farm of Totathaoig, near Glenvarragil House, about two miles from the church in Portree. This was quite a distance for an old man who only ever travelled by foot.

He died in 1799 aged ninety-two and the new minister was the Rev. Alexander Campbell, schoolmaster of Portree, who then moved from the schoolmaster's house at Kiltaraglen to Totathaoig. To emphasise the need for a manse he wrote to the Chamberlain describing the house as, 'that comfortless dwelling possessed by John Nicolson that was old and cold' and he requested compensation in cash. The Commissioners acknowledged, 'the unpleasantness of his situation without a fit place of worship or fixed abode'.

In 1811, when only forty-one years old, the Rev. Alexander Campbell died after a fall downstairs, leaving his wife with enormous debts. Keeping up the family tradition, Margaret Campbell wrote to Lord MacDonald about her situation and it was arranged that Hugh Bethune, the Ground Officer, would allocate a piece of ground on Shulishader farm to build a house so that she could send her children to school. Their father had probably taught them at home as it is a long way from Totathaoig to Kiltaraglen. In 1816 Mrs Campbell married Alexander MacLeod of Cuidrach.

Alexander Campbell's successor, the Rev. Coll MacDonald, compiler of the 'New Statistical Account', also lived in the 'comfortless house' at Totathaoig. Eventually, in 1820 a new church was built, almost a century after the first, on the village side of the burial ground. Over a century later it became the Black Memorial Hall, then 'Dovetail Furnishings' and is now being refurbished. A new manse was built at Pienmore, which was even further from the church than Totathaoig.

CHAPTER 4

Early Villagers

Many of the occupants of the first houses in the new village of Portree were incomers, who, having unusual names for this part of the country, stood out from the more usual MacDonalds and Nicolsons. They were tradesmen employed in building work and administrators. There were also local estate workers.

Some of the original residents of the area, tenants of Kiltaraglen and the cottars living along the edge of the bay, objected to the proposed new village. John Nicolson had a house and store by the shore and was afraid he would be asked to leave before the building began. Later he applied to set up as a merchant in the new village.

The Rev. Alexander Campbell though, by 1801 was no longer schoolmaster and was living at Totathaoig, still had some land on the old glebe. He was concerned that he would lose this ground if plans for the village went ahead. He decided to apply for land at Leasgeary instead.

To get his new village underway Lord MacDonald engaged the services of the architect James Gillespie as his Clerk of

Works or Architect Superintendent, as he was described in the Estate Papers. For almost twenty years he was responsible for building in Portree and Skye generally.

James Gillespie's wife, Mary Urquhart, came to Skye with him and their son, Archibald, was born here in 1803. After leaving Skye he remarried (we don't know what became of Mary). His new wife was an heiress called Margaret Graham, so he added Graham to his name to become the better known James Gillespie Graham. He began his career as a joiner and mason in Dunblane and worked himself up in his profession until he was recognised as an architect. He specialised in designing castellated country houses (Taymouth Castle in Perthshire), gothic churches (St Mary's Cathedral and St John Tollbooth, both in Edinburgh) and Prince Charlie's Monument at Glenfinnan. He became sufficiently proficient as an architect to enter a design for the new Houses of Parliament after the fire of 1843.

His first buildings in Portree, completed by 1800, were the courthouse and prison, the smithy, a coalyard and the pier. Before he started building, Lord MacDonald enquired into 'rules and regulations' for new villages. He did not want them to be too strict in case it discouraged the poorer people from settling there and asked his factor to enquire about the rules in force in other new villages. His concern with rules and regulations may be the reason why one of his first buildings was the prison. Inveraray and Cromarty also have prisons. There was at that time what the ruling class perceived to be a swelling wave of crime which led to transportation and eventually the colonisation of Australia. Though this was centred mainly in London and other large cities to the south, the fear of the 'criminal classes' seems to have spread north.

The pier was an important item for a fishing village and the first on Knox's list. A simple pier was built by constructing an embankment with a slipway at the end of it, alongside the Lump or Meall na h-Acairseid. In 1818 Thomas Telford designed a more sophisticated landing pier and wharf, not built till 1850. He suggested that there should be a protective levee of rubble stone placed to the south east of the existing pier to shelter the boating place and wharf which would cost £110.

To complete Knox's list, the first building to be put up near the pier, was at different times a store, a cooperage, accommodation to let and a private residence. It became part of Beaumont Crescent when that was built in 1839, and is now a hotel.

For an architect who became known later for his more pretentious designs, James Gillespie's buildings in Portree were very plain, as is his courthouse and jail, sometimes described as the oldest extant building in Portree. Like much of his work, it needed repairs and alterations soon after completion. The accountants complained that his initial estimates were 'not extravagant, but the cost of repairs and alterations were very high'.

The architect from Perthshire was evidently having problems with the wet and windy climate of Skye and the jail let in the rain. When Sheriff Frazer of Inverness-shire came to inspect the jail, 'to have it declared safe', he insisted that it be made watertight and the cells plastered. By 1802 Murdoch MacLeod, the jailer had still received no salary.

He was also very slow in presenting his accounts. In 1812 he was asked to state the cost of every building erected for Lord MacDonald 'without any further procrastination', but he was still being asked to give an account of money spent on Skye in 1815, and again in 1818.

James Gillespie's next project was a house for the new Chamberlain, Captain Duncan MacDougal. He took over when John Campbell of Lochend, who had come to Portree from the Breadalbane Estate, retired in 1805. Gillespie had designed the house that was to be built on the old glebe. Captain MacDougal was impatient for work to begin and frequently wrote to Lord MacDonald to enquire about the progress of the building. However, once the house, now Portree House, was finished in 1807 Captain MacDougal was outraged that as Factor, 'he should be required to live at or near Portree, a place not only disagreeable in itself but subject to an unavoidable expense'. So to support his large family the three farms of Balmeanach, Gedintailor and Pienchorran at Braes were leased to him as one farm. Later that same year Captain MacDougal died of lockjaw (tetanus), leaving his wife, Jane, with their eleven children. They stayed in the Chamberlain's house till Whitsun, while her oldest son, Alexander, took over the lease of the farm for a year before taking a farm at Ardentrive, on Kerrera.

While the Chamberlain's house was under construction, work had been going ahead, as it had since 1804, on ordinary village houses – though according to the 1810 map of Portree there had not been much progress. Some of the stone for building the village houses was shipped from Raasay. It was also quarried more conveniently from the Lump and from Shullishadder. To the south of the Wool Mill and through 'Sleepy,' behind the High School, evidence of the old quarry workings can still be seen under the growth of hazel and rowan and more modern garden shrubs.

The village houses were let by the room:-

Rental of the New Houses at Portree-Whitsun 1809–1810

Rooms

1 – Malcolm Wright

2 –

3 – Angus MacDonald

4 –

5 –

6 – Lachlan MacKinnon, Eig & Rasay

7 –

8 – Malcolm MacLeod, Postmaster

9 –

10, 11, 12 – Occupied by masons and carpenters

Arrears due from Angus MacDonald	£3
Received from Malcolm Wright rent of one room for 1807–1808	£8
Received from Angus MacDonald rent of one room for 1808 –	£4

26th November 1810, Correct Rental of New Houses at Portroo

John MacPherson
Chamberlain

Malcolm Wright, writer or lawyer and Sheriff Clerk of Portree, moved from his room in the new village and took over the lease of Kiltaraglen House (the former school house?). What he did in 1810 to deserve the condemnation of Lord MacDonald's Commissioners we will never know, as the details of the case seem to have been destroyed at the time. The following is an extract from the MacDonald Estate Papers:

> During the many years Lord Macdonald's Commissioners have superintended his Lordship's affairs, nothing of so vile a nature has come under their consideration as Mr Wright's low tampering, with poor, ignorant and illiterate men, for the heinous purpose of destroying the good name of a neighbour, and that too in aggravation of the offence, for the mean purpose of promoting his own worldly interests at the expense of the character another man. His Lordship's Commissioners are at a loss to express their detestation of such a deliberate and unprovoked wickedness, but they direct in the most positive manner that the Chamberlain shall never employ Mr Wright in any law business, and that he shall, as much as may be in his power, prevent his being employed by any of Lord Macdonald's tenantry, and they shall be glad how soon this person quits Lord Macdonald's property, to whom no encouragement or countenance of any kind is to be shown by Lord Macdonald's Chamberlain.
>
> Although James Ferguson's conduct in this shameful business is not so culpable as Mr Wright's, yet it proves him to be worse than indiscreet, and a person would not stick at trifles to injure a man against whom he had conceived a grudge.

He also was to be dismissed.

As the Commissioners hoped, Malcolm Wright seems to have left Portree, as neither he nor any descendants appear in either the Parish or Estate Records.

Angus MacDonald, who was a Messenger, had earlier shared a room with John MacLean, a merchant. Both appear in the 1841 census, Angus as a seventy-five year old agricultural labourer and John, sixty years old and independent.

Malcolm MacLeod was the Portree postmaster of the newly established postal service on Skye when the best routes for the postal 'runners' carrying the mails across the island had been worked out. Later Post Offices were set up in Portree, Dunvegan, Sconser, (the new road from Portree to Sconser was opened in 1815) Kylerhea and Glenelg. The Kylerhea crossing was the main route from Skye before the regular boat service from Portree to Lochcarron connected with the train from Inverness. The railway line from Dingwall to Strome Ferry was opened in August 1870.

Lachlan MacKinnon was a house carpenter from Eigg who married Marjorie MacLean from Fort Augustus. They had three daughters, Mary, the oldest, was born in 1828. They were still living in Bosville Terrace in 1851.

There were many masons, carpenters and other tradesmen who could have occupied Rooms 10, 11 and 12. Malcolm Coldstream, James Gillespie's cousin and agent in Dunblane, engaged workmen – masons, wrights and quarriers – for him and arranged payment for their wives who remained in Dunblane.

There were masons; John Henderson who took charge of freighting stone from Raasay and Peter Ferguson who built the wall round the Chamberlain's house. There was a joiner, Robert Frazer, George MacIssac, a slater (slated houses would have been a novelty in Portree then) and George Douglas, a plumber who fitted the lead on the slated roofs. They all appear to have come to Portree to work and left without becoming involved in the local community. It has been suggested that, before they left, they may have trained the local builders in the use of dressed stone and slates – not their usual materials.

Others did not leave immediately. Duncan MacCallum, the smith, stayed long enough to marry Flora Finlayson from Kenkreggan near Sconser in 1811 and was still in Portree in 1821 when their third child was born. However in the 1841 census there is no sign of Mrs MacCallum and her family, and the only Duncan MacCallum is a handloom weaver rather than a smith.

Similarly, James Ferguson, a joiner from Callander who was James Gillespie's foreman, married Sybella MacCrimmond from Bracadale. With the security of a steady job and regular income, they had a large family – six girls and three boys. He was involved in Malcolm Wright's disgrace and as his conduct was described by the Commissioners as 'worse than indiscrete'. They expected James Gillespie to dismiss him. James Gillespie did not. Their youngest son was named Gillespie, possibly in recognition of this. Their oldest daughter, Mary Ann, married Portree baker Duncan Frazer in 1833 and they emigrated to New Zealand. The Fergusons, though not the whole family, were still living at Goitrein na Creige, now Viewfield, in 1851. There are the ruined remains of two houses beside the path through the trees above the Aros Centre. One of these may have been the Ferguson house.

It is possible that Peter MacGregor from Argyll, though not a construction worker, was already known to James Gillespie. He wrote to Lord MacDonald from Perth where he was studying classics, mathematics and bookkeeping with a private tutor, asking for employment. Whether Lord MacDonald employed him or not, Peter MacGregor came to Skye and in 1831 married

Margaret MacNeil from Stornoway. He became an agricultural labourer and crofter at Goirtein na Creige where they brought up a family of seven children.

The Chamberlain of 1810 was John MacPherson. Though he applied for the position of Chamberlain after the death of Captain MacDougal, Lord MacDonald did not appoint him till after the death of Colonel Graham, Captain MacDougal's successor. John MacPherson was not a very sympathetic chamberlain. When Lord MacDonald's Trustees had voted for a rent reduction to counter the bad publicity after a report of large scale emigration from Skye, John MacPherson protested: 'Giving a deduction of rent, in my opinion was the worst plan that could have been fallen on, and beneath the dignity of Lord MacDonald to yield to a few restless infatuated people'. While he was prepared to let land to some of the best tenants who intended to emigrate, he did not know how to deal with Skye's surplus population.

The oldest of his four sons was called Robert Alexander Wentworth, either in honour of his landlord and employer Lord MacDonald, or because his wife, Christine MacDonald, may have been a member of Lord MacDonald's family. Alexander, 1st Lord MacDonald had married Elizabeth Diana, daughter of Godfrey and Diana Bosville of Gunthwaite and Thorpe Hall in Yorkshire. Her mother was the daughter of Sir William Wentworth of Bretton. Their oldest son, the 2nd Lord, was called Alexander Wentworth MacDonald. His brother, Godfrey, took the name Bosville as he was to inherit the English estates, but when Sir Alexander died unmarried Godfrey reverted to MacDonald and became the 3rd Lord. In recognition of their English connections, the first streets of the new village were called Wentworth Street and Bosville Terrace.

CHAPTER 5

Building Continues

Despite all the building work that had been carried out in Portree by 1810, plans for a settlement there had still not been finalised. Lord MacDonald emphasised that if the plans were to go ahead, building costs should not exceed £400, which seems very little even for 1810. He had James Gillespie draw up plans for an alternative fishing village at Kyleakin, to be called New Liverpool, but they were too elaborate and would have been even more costly.

After much talking and persuading a new school was built in the centre of the village in what was to become the main street. The new church at Portree, which was to be a 'simple, respectable building of hewn stone to contain 600 persons', was completed in 1820, and a manse for the minister was built across Portree Bay at Pienmore.

Just before the estate survey was carried out in 1830 the National Bank of Scotland, now the Royal Bank of Scotland, leased half an acre of land between the new church and the courthouse and jail to build a bank, with accommodation for the bank agent. This, the village's first commercial building, was suitably imposing with a bow window on both floors to the front and a stained glass window at the side.

Portree was now definitely a village with its new church, school and bank. The church, having been there before the bank, gave its name to the street running past the inn – Church Street, though it was later changed to Bank Street.

Wentworth Street, simply 'The Street' on the 1830 map, was taking shape from the Church/Bank Street end. It was proposed to extend it towards the Chamberlain's House, well beyond where it stops now in the Square. According to the 1830 map, there was to be no square. Where Bridge Road (constructed about 1815 as Parliamentary Road), joined Wentworth Street, was to be built over. Between Wentworth Street and the Green and on the other side of Wentworth Street there were to be gardens or allotments, presumably to supplement the income from fishing, as in the British Fisheries Society villages.

But, in the 1860s, the new Courthouse, sited beside the newly built jail, and the North of Scotland Bank (now the Clydesdale Bank) both designed by architects Mathew and Laurie, were positioned on either side of the Parliamentary Road instead of following the proposed street plans. They were both impressive buildings. The Courthouse, solid and square with decorative urns at the corners of the roof, and though in line with the existing street, faced inwards. The bank, facing the courthouse, was more like a Victorian suburban house than a bank, with its own suburban garden. The National Bank, after all, only had a back garden.

In the 1870s the Caledonian Bank (now the Bank of Scotland), another imposing building within its own garden, was built in line with the first one, leaving enough room for Hawthorn Cottage (now the Bakery) in between. This formed

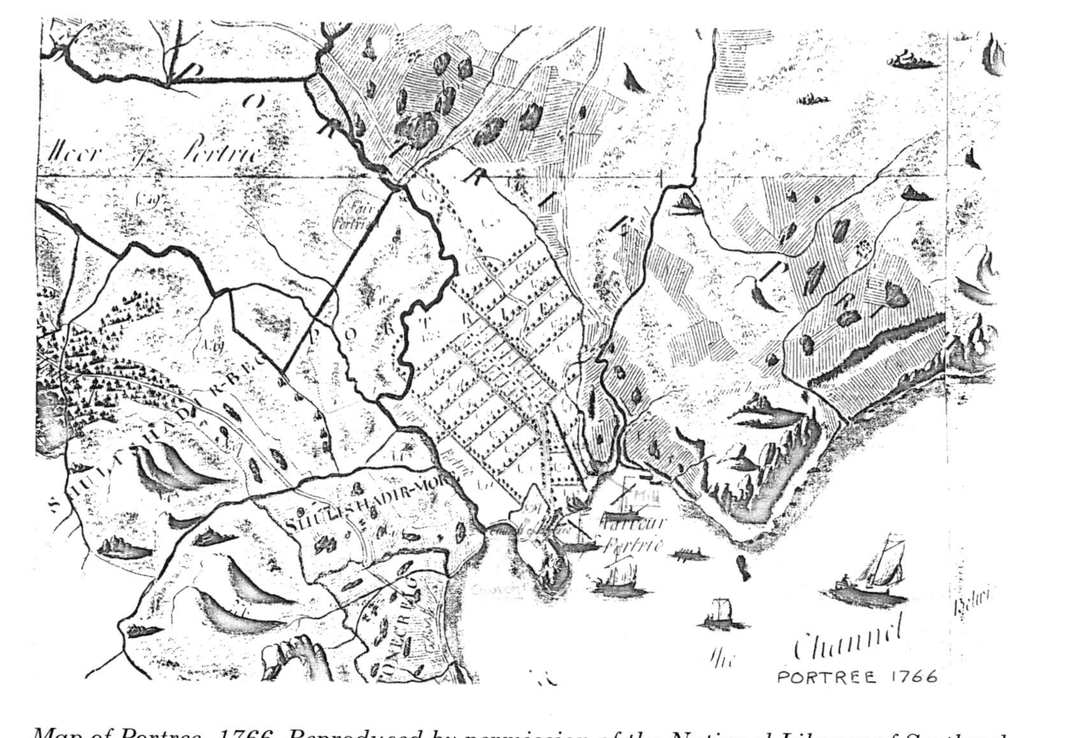

Map of Portree, 1766. Reproduced by permission of the National Library of Scotland

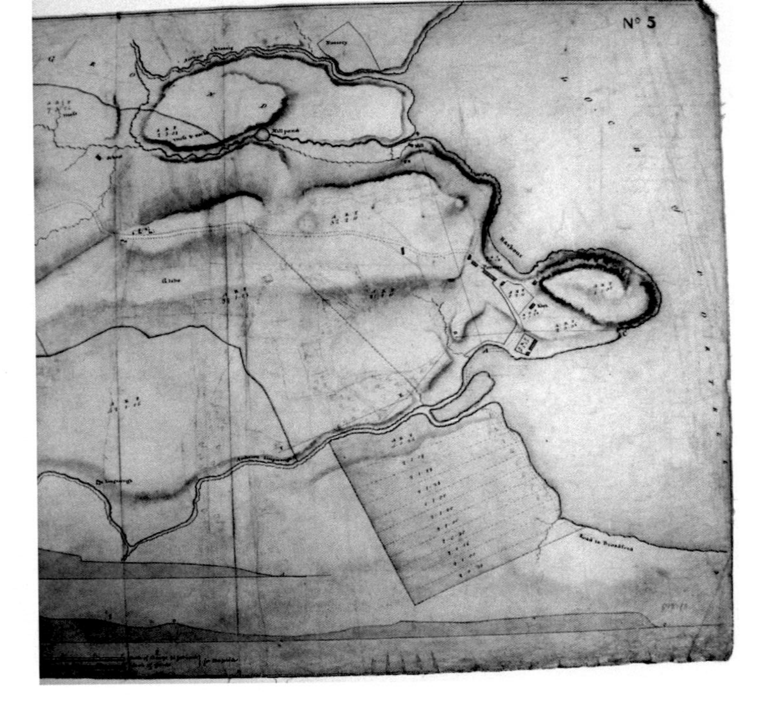

Map of Portree, 1810. From the collections of the Museum of the Isles.
© Clan Donald Lands Trust

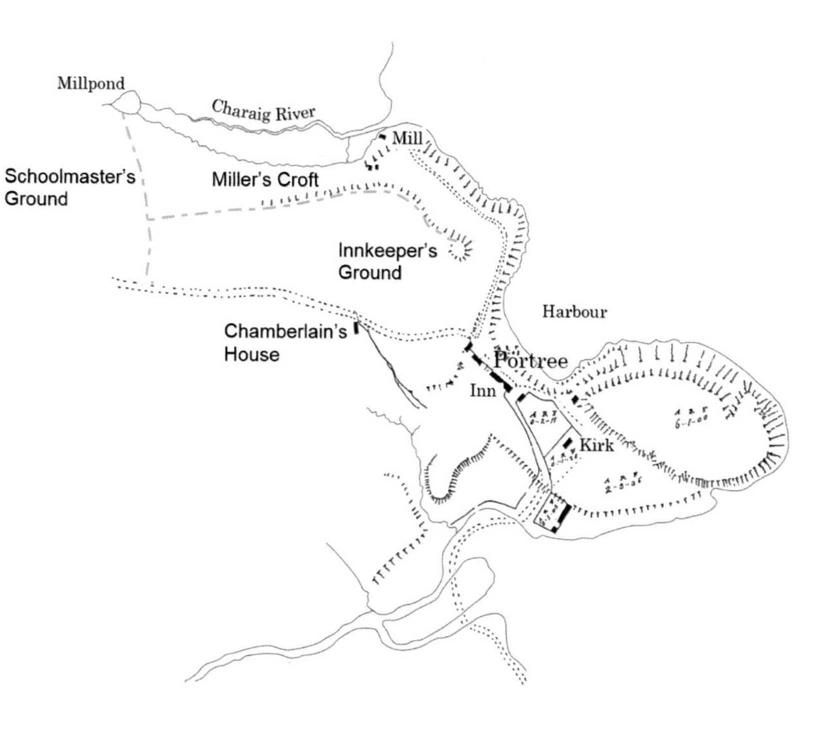

Annotated version of 1810 map

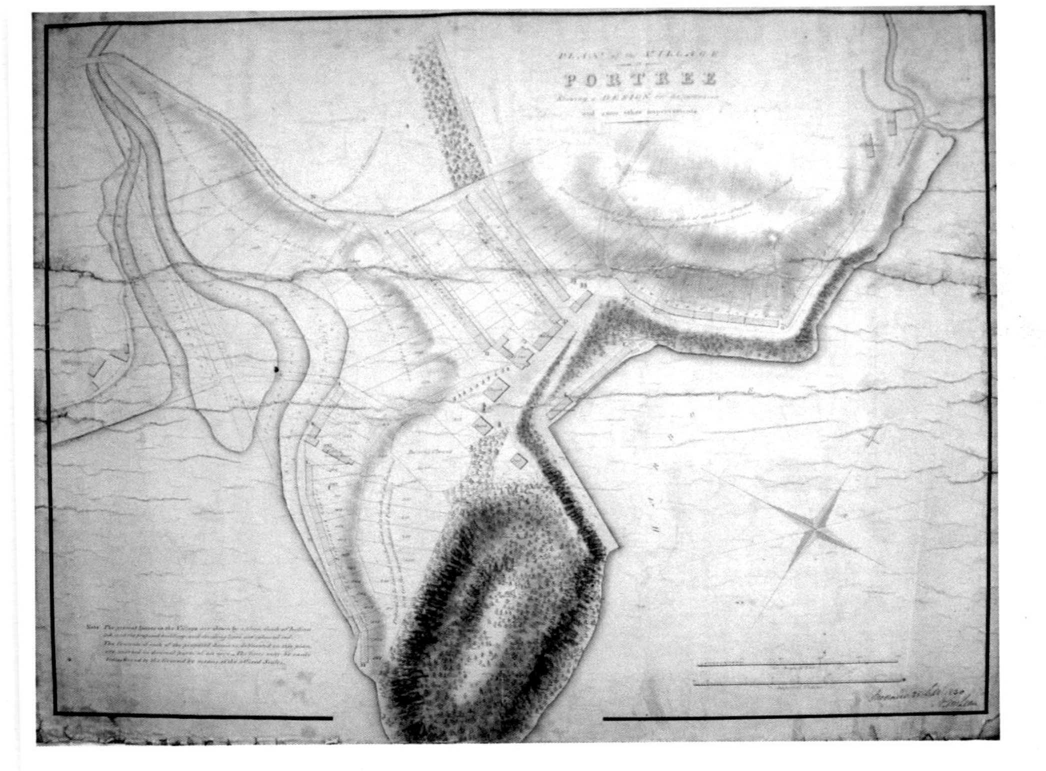

Plan of the village of Portree, 1830. From the collections of the Museum of the Isles. © Clan Donald Lands Trust

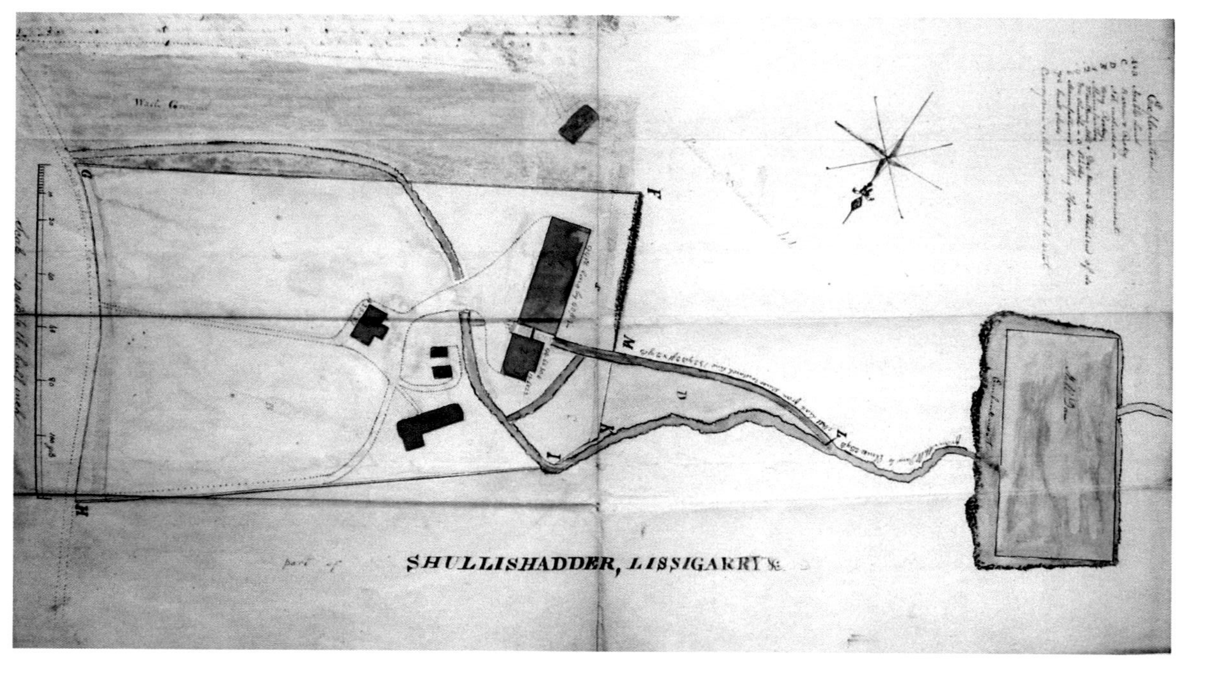

The Wool Mill, Portree, 1848. From the collections of the Museum of the Isles.
© Clan Donald Lands Trust

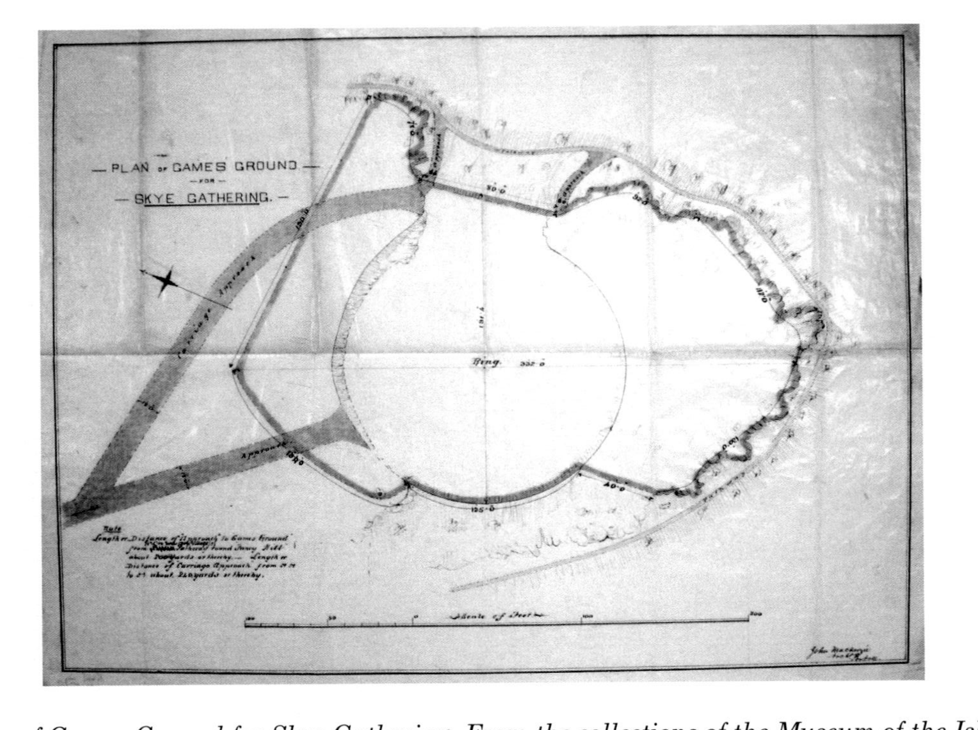

Plan of Games Ground for Skye Gathering. From the collections of the Museum of the Isles.
© Clan Donald Lands Trust

REVISING FOR THE SECOND EDITION.
Alexander, 1st Lord Macdonald, and James Boswell.
From a contemporary caricature.

Sir Alexander and Boswell Cartoon

The Skye Gathering Hall and the old prison above Quay Street and Douglas Row with Fancy Hill, 'the Lump' behind

Games Day in the original arena 'up the Lump'

Somerled Square with a tour coach in front of the Court House, the Clydesdale Bank, the Bakery and the Bank of Scotland

Beaumont Crescent down by the shore with Bosville Terrace above

Bank Street showing the Skye Gathering Hall, the old prison and the Royal Bank of Scotland

Portree House, The Chamberlain's House

A winter view of Portree from Suidh' Fhinn, Fingal's Seat

the second side of the Square. Directly opposite, Portree Hotel made up the third side. Though Lord MacDonald may have expected and even preferred the proposed longer main street, (or more likely did not care one way or another) he gave the newly formed Square his approval by naming it for his ancestor, Somerled, Lord of the Isles, but as it was not named immediately, it may have been in honour of Somerled, the 5th Lord Macdonald. For many years it was simply known as Jail Square.

The Parliamentary Road continued to cross the Square diagonally. Even when the War Memorial was erected in the centre of the Square after the First World War, the traffic to and from Wentworth Street simply passed up one side of it and down the other. It is only since the Square was pedestrianised that the traffic has had to go round the edges, rather than heading straight to Wentworth Street.

Overlooking the harbour, on the 1830 map, was the 'New Row of Houses' to be named Bosville Terrace. The proposed extension to this street was built, and as it was on the Miller's croft, was called Mill Road.

The first house in Bosville Terrace, a plain three storey house (now part of the Bosville Restaurant) was in use as the North of Scotland Bank before the new Bank was built in the Square. In the 1841 census the principal house holder and banker was Kenneth MacAskill and his lodger, Laurence Skene from Aberdeenshire, was the bank clerk. Ten years later in 1851, Kenneth MacAskill was listed as a Distiller (at Talisker Distillery), Laurence Skene, still the lodger, was the bank agent and the new bank clerk was Kenneth MacAskill's nephew, William Tolmie.

In 1855 Laurence Skene married William Tolmie's sister, Jane Campbell Tolmie. At first they lived at Scorrybreck House, which had been built for the tenant of Scorrybreck farm by the MacDonald Estate in 1850, where their four oldest children were born. They moved along the shore to Redcliff, where three more children were born. By the time their youngest child was born they had finally moved to the North of Scotland Bank House in the Square. Skene's oldest son, Thomas, also became bank agent there, so that by the 1880s this bank was known locally as Skene's Bank. Another son, Laurence, was a solicitor and the Procurator Fiscal for Skye and became Hon. Treasurer of Skye Shinty Club in 1898.

Down at sea level, at the head of the bay, another row of houses was proposed beside the storehouse/cooperage. Beaumont Crescent, as it was to be called, was designed by Thomas Telford and built, starting in 1839, from the stone quarried from the nearby Sron nan Cudaigean, or Cuddy Point. The Honourable Susan, daughter of Godfrey, Lord MacDonald, had married Commander Richard Beaumont in 1831. He had leased the strip of land that the houses were built on, and gave the Crescent its name. Thirty-two families were living in Beaumont Crescent in 1851.

Besides the earlier occupants of the village – bankers, lawyers and construction workers – businesses were being established in the village. Merchants, grocers or shopkeepers (their own description of their occupations from the census) were applying to the factor for premises or building sites for their shops. Both William Cumming and later, Alexander MacNaughton, who came from Ardnamurchan and lived in Beaumont Crescent, wanted premises on the Quay area to supply the growing population there.

By 1841 there were eleven merchants (grocers, butchers, drapers or just shopkeepers) in the village. There were also seven dressmakers, six tailors, nine shoemakers, one watchmaker and one saddle maker. The village seemed to attract merchants and tradesmen, not only from Skye but from the mainland as well.

Wentworth Street 1851 –

Peter MacDonald	Merchant	Kilmuir
Dougal MacMillan	Joiner	Strath
Angus MacPherson	Boatman	Portree
George MacLeod	Gardener	Golspie
John MacDonald	Gardener	Bracadale
David Simpson	Watchmaker	Murray
William Ferguson	Tailor	Uinish
William Brown	Wool carder	Aberdeen
Murdo MacDonald	Teacher	Lochcarron
Duncan Cameron	Merchant	Lochleven
Neil Nicolson	Grocer	Portree
Daniel Duncan	Baker	Galloway
Malcolm Cameron	Grocer/draper	Kirkhill
James MacIntyre	Merchant/draper/grocer	Portree

Wentworth Street continued to expand as other merchants arrived, such as William MacRae, who was let ground in 1862 for premises which were to be built of stone at a cost of £300.

John MacPherson's successor as Chamberlain, Dr. Alexander MacLeod, did much to further the development of the village. He has been remembered on Skye as a sympathetic and humanitarian factor and doctor.

On a visit to North Uist, which was still owned by the MacDonalds in 1824, Lord MacDonald first met Dr. MacLeod, or Dr. Ban, as he was generally known. He had taken over the medical duties in North Uist from his father, Dr. Murdoch MacLeod of Kilpheder, a descendant of the MacLeods of Rigg. Dr. Murdoch had been an army surgeon in the American War of Independence and three of his sons, including Alexander, were doctors.

Lord MacDonald was so impressed, not only by the medical skills of Dr. MacLeod, but by his engineering abilities – he had stabilised the sand dunes by planting them with marram grass, and drained Loch Scolpaig (which is still there though perhaps reduced in size), one of the many lochs on North Uist, to provide the crofters with more arable land – that he asked him to come to Skye as Chamberlain.

On Skye he managed to drain Loch Chaluim Chille, in Kilmuir, previous attempts having been unsuccessful, leaving good arable land. It was promptly taken from the crofters and added to an already large sheep farm. He had also hoped to drain the Moss of Portree to produce more arable land, and to plant trees for shelter. In the village he planned to provide the fishermen living round the bay with a quarter of an acre of land each, to supplement their income from fishing, and he succeeded as can be seen on the 1830 map. Also a George Washington Wilson photograph of c. 1900 shows two men and two women carrying seaweed for fertilizer and planting potatoes in one of the quarter acre fields at Bayfield.

He also had plans to encourage tourists to visit Portree. To improve the amenities, he planted the Meall (or the Lump) with trees (Corsican Pines) and shrubs so that it then became known as Fancy Hill. Above the pier he built a small tower or folly, which has recently been renovated. It is thought that it was intended as a signal to ships in the harbour that there was a doctor and medical supplies available on shore. If a tower was generally recognized by seamen as an indication of medical assistance, where are the other towers? There is one at Scolpaig in North Uist, again the creation of Dr. MacLeod when he was factor there, but it was built as part of a scheme to provide employment during the potato famine. It has also been suggested that it was this tower or folly that inspired the name Fancy Hill.

In 1825 with Lord MacDonald's agreement, Dr. MacLeod arranged the first Skye Games to 'bring some brightness into the lives of the ordinary people'. The arena, which is still used for the modern Highland Games, was formed when stone was quarried from the Lump – and here there is conflicting information – either at the time of Dr. Ban's Games or after his grandson Harry MacDonald of Viewfield and his associates revived the Games in 1877. Or perhaps one began the job and the other completed it. The stone was used to build some of the houses in the village, and the Skye Gathering Hall. However the red sandstone used in the building of the Hall did not come from the Lump. Harry MacDonald had instigated the Skye Gatherings as a 'secular replacement for the Holy Friars'. He apparently did not appreciate the new Free Church.

For the expected tourists, Dr. Ban envisaged bathing huts along the shore, but that was never put into practice. Even though the shore would have been a lot cleaner in the 19th century than it is now, it could never have been considered an attractive beach.

Dr. MacLeod was a much more sympathetic factor than his predecessor and never pressed needy tenants for the rent or even considered eviction when a bad harvest made payment impossible. When he was factor he never charged for any medical services. On the death of Lord MacDonald in 1832, he returned to North Uist as factor for the new owner, Colonel Gordon of Cluny, but came back to Portree as doctor in 1851.

In 1815 he had married Mary, daughter of Kenneth Campbell of Strond, a descendant of Donald MacLeod of Bernera, better known as 'The Old Trojan'. They had two sons. Donald, following family tradition, was a doctor, and Murdoch, before emigrating to Australia, was a bank clerk in Portree (with his brother-in-law at the National Bank?). Of their four daughters, two married ministers; one in North Uist and the other, the Rev. John MacIver of Kilmuir. Their third daughter, Johanna, married Harry MacDonald, a lawyer from Dingwall who is said to have been so poor he walked all the way to Portree. He became bank agent for the National Bank in Portree and when the Portree postmaster was having problems with his accounts, took over as postmaster as well.

Though still living above the Bank in 1851, Harry MacDonald was granted ground in 1845 for building a house at Viewfield. This is the first reference to Viewfield rather than Goirtein na Creige. In the 1854 Estate Rents the house is listed as 'Viewfield Cottage and Park', but was later enlarged to become Viewfield House. It is still in the same family and run as a hotel.

Their oldest son, Alexander, was the MacDonald Estate factor at the time of the Battle of Braes in 1882. He also managed five other Skye estates. He was bank agent, Skye's only lawyer, principal collector of rates and taxes, member and clerk of the school board in six parishes, and captain of the Portree Volunteers. He was known to the crofters as The Uncrowned King of Skye, and to the Scottish Office as Pooh Bah – Lord High Everything Else (from Gilbert and Sullivan's *Mikado*).

Alexander was in reality quite sympathetic to the situation of the crofters, but any generous act was regarded as the influence of his grandfather, not of his father. In his book *The Former Days* Dr. Norman MacLean quotes his mother:

> Harry was a poor man when he came to Portree, apparently walking most of the way. Dr. Ban was factor then, and Harry made up his mind to marry one of his many daughters. He did not marry money as much as marry where money was. As the factor's son-in-law all the MacDonald Estate money came to his bank and all the Estate law business came to his office. Soon he was the most prosperous man on the Island, unlike his father-in-law who never expected to get paid for medical attentions and gave what he could to those in need.

Mrs MacLean concluded, 'This Island never saw a doctor so wise, so clever, so humane as an Dotair Ban, or one who lived so humbly towards God and so justly and so mercifully towards his fellows.'

Then, in 1854, Lord MacDonald asked him to take over the medical duties in Strath, Sleat and Knoydart. Returning one night from visiting a patient in Knoydart, he missed the path, fell over a sixty foot cliff and died from his injuries. He was buried in North Uist.

CHAPTER 6

Destitution, Emigration or Industry

Alexander Campbell insisted in the Old Statistical Account for Portree that there had been no emigration from the Parish of Portree, but this was not strictly correct. It was to stem the flow of people leaving the island and 'wandering the world', that Lord MacDonald had decided to create his fishing village at the Harbour of Portree. In 1772 Boswell describes the ship, the *Nestor*, at anchor in Portree Bay, waiting to take on emigrants bound for America. Johnson had gone on board and reported that the accommodation for the emigrants was very good: 'A row of beds down each side of a ward, the same size every way and fit to contain four people'. Perhaps he would not have been so much in favour if he were to have been one of these four.

In the New Statistical Account for Portree of 1841 the Rev. Coll MacDonald reported that in spite of the numbers of emigrants having risen by 500–600 the previous year, the population was rising. This was in part due to the introduction of inoculation, mainly against smallpox. He also said that though the fishing had been plentiful earlier – fish had been cured in Portree and dispatched to Glasgow and London – by

1841 there was no fishing of any consequence. The small plots of land were not enough to keep a family, especially when they were subdivided among the family to provide land for their sons. The highest praise, he wrote, is due to Lord MacDonald for his liberality: '...having this last year expended large sums of money in conveying the poor people on his property to North America.' Well, the minister appointed by Lord MacDonald would say that, wouldn't he?

Perhaps Lord MacDonald would have spent no more money by allocating a little more of his property to 'the poor people', to enable them to make a decent living. He would still have their rents coming in instead of them being in arrears and he would not have had to pay for their poor relief.

This passage from Fenyo Krisztina's *Contempt, Sympathy and Romance* says it all:

> What the landlords were really afraid of was the new poor law provision, which would put the burden of sustaining the able-bodied poor on the owners of the land. To avoid this 'ruinous result of their own oppression and short-sighted rapacity' [Mulock – newspaper reporter] the Highland landowners were determined to expatriate the people from their lands. This was the real motive behind the emigration policies.

In the middle of the 19th century the potato crop failed and, as the diet consisted mainly of potatoes, there was widespread famine. The transportation of convicts to Australia came to an end when gold was found there in large quantities. Transporting them to a country where they had a chance, albeit a slim one, of becoming rich did not seem sufficient punishment, so the transport ships were re-employed shipping emigrants there instead.

Many from Skye left for Australia and New Zealand, including some, according to the boat lists, from Portree. Some of these may only be listed as from Portree because they lived there while waiting for an emigration ship, as they are not recorded in the parish records or census returns. John MacQueen, listed as coming from Portree though actually from 'MacLeod country', had worked as an agricultural labourer at Goirtein na Creige for some years before emigrating. He had married a servant of John Ross, the Innkeeper, and they had one child. Like many other emigrants at that time, they could pay very little towards their passage and had to be outfitted for their journey. Ballingall, the factor involved in the eviction of the people from Suishnish and Borreraig, thought that since John MacQueen had a boat he should be able to pay his way.

More established Portree families emigrated too. Donald MacDonald, a gardener (the census does not indicate where he worked or for whom, though there was a walled garden at the Chamberlain's house) sailed for Australia on the *Araminta* in 1852 with his wife Marion and their large family of four sons and four daughters (aged six to twenty-three) and a grandson born to their oldest daughter, Mary, on the voyage. Their passage cost him £35.

The following year the Portree postman, Angus Kelly, left for Australia with his wife Flora and their family of two sons and three daughters (aged twelve to twenty-two) on board the notorious *Hercules*. Though they were described as a very poor family they had promised to pay £27.3s.1d towards their passage. Being a postman must have been a part time job as he was reported to have been a good labourer.

To feed those who were unable to or chose not to emigrate, extra meal had to be provided. The original government plan was that landlords should distribute the meal as wages to crofters employed in road-making or drainage schemes.

Godfrey, 4th Lord MacDonald, described by Major Haliday, the officer in charge of the Portree meal depot, as one of the worst landlords, agreed to employ some of his destitute tenants in a government funded drainage scheme, but due to a lack of commitment nothing was organised or carried out properly. The drainage scheme only employed a fraction of the crofters in need of assistance and lasted only a matter of weeks. The meal to be used as wages was sold at a profit by the factor, Ballingal, on the way back to Skye. When the outlying crofters trekked into Portree for their meal ration there was very little for them.

By 1852 Lord MacDonald had not paid Alexander Cameron, the Portree meal merchant, for the meal he had supplied to the Board for the Relief of Destitute in the Highlands and Islands. The Board's relief officer, Duncan Cameron, among others, had received no salary.

Industry was seen to be the answer – either reviving old ones like fishing or inventing new ones. In Portree the new industry was to be a wool carding and spinning factory. The building of this mill was to be financed from the remains of a fund collected for destitute Highlanders by the Destitution Board. The Wool Mill was built in 1848 on five acres of ground at the northern end of the Shuillishadder stone quarry (more a layer of rock removed from about a quarter of a mile of hillside than a quarry) beside the Lon na h-Atha. Lon na h-Atha is a tributary of the Leasgeary River and was the mill's original source of power.

Initially water to turn the mill wheel was brought by a series of sluices and lades from a mill dam further up the hillside. Later a small mill pond was constructed behind mill to help control the flow of water (in the mid-1990s, the dam was declared derelict, pumped out, filled in and turned into a shinty pitch. This small wildlife haven was missed by many. To save the smaller millpond from a similar fate it was cleaned out, and paths and bridges constructed, with the help of a band of school children) and in 1882 a new 30hp engine was brought to Portree and installed by the mechanics of a 'well known Glasgow firm'.

If Harry MacDonald of the National Bank had cornered all the Estate business, Laurence Skene of the North of Scotland Bank, having married into another influential family, had his finger in many of the remaining pies. While Samuel Hogg, a businessman and hosiery manufacturer from Aberdeen, took over the management of the Mill, Laurence Skene, also from Aberdeen, as agent for the Trustees (of the North of Scotland Bank,) looked after the financial side of the business. Because of this he was frequently designated 'Mill-owner'. The wool carder, William Brown, living in Wentworth Street, came from Aberdeen too and it was he who was called in to witness, along with Skene and Hogg, any Mill business transactions. He eventually took over from Hogg as Woollen Manufacturer. Could these three have known each other before they came to Portree?

The purpose of the Mill was to give employment to the destitute of the village and Skye generally, but working there were the wool carder, William Brown and his lodger, a wool spinner called Alexander Glenny (definitely not local). Even Samuel Hogg's eighteen-year-old son was employed as a weaver.

However up to twenty women also worked there, some as wool twisters like Catherine MacIntosh and Elizabeth Buchanan of Shulishader, while others sorted the raw wool. Over a thousand others worked at home knitting stockings, socks, gloves, shirts, comforters and drawers for the Glasgow market.

Hogg took on any knitters who wanted employment within a twenty-four-mile radius, essentially anywhere north of the Cuillins. He distributed the wool and collected the made up garments at his own expense – which is just as well as, to fulfil his orders, crofter's wives had to knit all the time, even when carrying loaded creels on their backs. Even then, they earned only a penny a day. And the profits, Lady MacAskill and Dr. Jim Hunter tell us, went into the pockets of a man who, thanks to the Destitution Board, had not even had to capitalise their return.

Lady MacAskill, while on Skye in 1851, visited the mill, which she said was beside the school. But the village school was not moved from Wentworth St to its present site at Shulishadder till 1875, so where was Lady MacAskill's school?

The Shulishader Lissigarry map of the mill shows the building across the Lon na h-Atha as a 'Free Church', with 'Stables' as a lean-to at the back. This building was used as the mill show room and store till the mill stopped production in the 1970s and the factory was converted to a shop. The only evidence of the stables now is a line along the wall above the windows. In the 1854 Rent Lists it appears as Portree Smithy and Free Church Stance. It is of an old-fashioned church design with an outside staircase to the gallery. There is another old building of similar design near Dunvegan Castle which was once used as a church and a school and is now used as a byre and hayloft. There is also one on Colonsay where the women of the congregation were expected to use the outside stairway to the gallery.

After the Disruption of 1843 many new churches were built, particularly Free Churches with their own schools so this building may have been used as a church school at the time of Lady MacAskill's visit. The Free Church, along with the Destitution Committees, was active in providing relief during the famine, which could be one reason why the mill was sited beside Free Church stance. This old Free Church, which for years stood empty with windows broken and under threat of demolition, has been given a new lease of life as a bakery (The Isle of Skye Baking Company).

Directly opposite the factory was the 'Manufacturer's Dwelling House 'and was the Manager's House till the mill closed completely. Keeping the Aberdeen connection it is called Bon Accord Cottage.

Victoria Cottage, 'to the east of Hogg's mill' was built in 1849 for Miss Christy MacAskill, a relative of the MacAskills living in the North of Scotland Bank House in Bosville Terrace. When she died in 1860 her sister Jessie MacAskill from Dunvegan inherited the cottage but gave up the lease, assigning it to Laurence Skene on payment of £100 for renouncing eighty years of a ninety-nine year lease. She died in Vaten in 1874.

Down the road in Heath cottage were Mary MacAskill and other members of the Isle of Eigg branch of the family. She was the aunt of Kenneth MacAskill of Bosville Terrace and Talisker

Distillery and died in 1866. In 1896 Heath Cottage was taken over by the Rev. George J. Smith, Bishop of Argyll and the Isles, when it was converted to a very small chapel. It has since been demolished to make room for a larger purpose built one, which in its turn was demolished in 2005 to be replaced by an even larger chapel.

Plans were drawn up in 1859 by architects Ross and Joass for the Parochial Boards of Skye for a Union or Combination Poor House. It was to be sited near the Wool Mill and ideally would give the mill a steady supply of workers. In 1863 a substantial house was built in a walled garden suitable for growing vegetables, but things did not go as planned. Of the nineteen inmates in the 1871 census not one was a mill worker. There were six children of whom three appeared to be orphans. There were two agricultural labourers, a dairymaid and assorted domestic servants.

Vegetables were still grown there when it was converted in 1922 to the Margaret Carnegie Hostel for girls attending the secondary school in Portree. (It is soon to be demolished to make way for a new Gaelic school.) The boys, a decade later, enjoyed a purpose built hostel like a French chateau (the Elgin Hostel), right beside the school, while the girls still had to walk up and down that road twice a day in all weathers!

Towards the end of the 19th century local mill workers must have been scarce as mill cottages became necessary. Two semi-detached houses, the beginning of a row of mill houses, were designed by John MacKenzie of Portree in 1889, though only one, Hazel Cottage, was ever built. It was sited below the mill where the river flows round the debris from the old quarry.

This was where stone was quarried to build the village. Until the mill closed in the 1970s, Hazel Cottage alternated with Bon Accord Cottage as the mill manager's house.

And so:

- Kiltaraglen was not the ancient name for the village before the arrival of the king.
- On old maps Portree appears as Portray or Portrie, but never Portrigh.
- Its name is descriptive and has nothing to do with the visit of any king.
- Sir James MacDonald may have wanted to build a village at Portree, but he didn't.
- It was not even chosen as an ideal site for a British Fisheries Society fishing village.

But within fifty years Portree grew from a few cottars' and fishermen's wee thatched houses round the Bay, and tenants working their bit of ground further inland at Kiltaraglen (and, of course, the mill, church and inn) to a thriving village. A real village with streets and slate roofed houses where people came from all over the island and from the mainland to set up in business – bakers and grocers, dressmakers and shoemaker and even a watchmaker, as well as the masons and carpenters essential for building a brand new village. Banks opened, lawyers, writers, clerks and civil servants arrived, attracted by the up and coming village. In spite of, or because of emigration (enforced or otherwise), industry came. The wool mill may have been started to counteract the effect of famine but it continued to process wool for over a hundred years.

Bibliography

Manuscript Sources:

Aitchison N. *MacBeth, Man and Myth* 1999

Bumstead J.M. *The People's Clearance*

Boswell J. *Journal of a Tour to the Hebrides* 1785

Cooper D. *Skye* 1970

Cooper D. *Skye Remembered*

Dogshon R. *The Age of the Clans* 2002

Dunlop J. *The British Fisheries Society 1786–1893*

Fenyo Krisztina *Contempt, Sympathy and Romance* 2000

Ferguson M. *Rambles in Skye* 1882

Haldane A.R.B. *The Drove Roads of Scotland* 1952

Hughes Robert *The Fatal Shore* 1987

Hunter J. *The Making of the Crofting Community* 1976

MacDonald I. A *Family in Skye 1908–1916* 1980

MacIntyre J. *Castles of Skye* 1938

MacKenzie H.H. *MacKenzie of Balone* 1941

MacLean A. *Old Skye Tales*

MacLean Allan *Telford's Highland Churches* 1989

MacLean N. *The Former Days* 1945

MacLeod F. *Togail Tir Marking Time* 1989

MacLeod R.H. *Flora MacDonald* 1995

Murray W.H. *The Islands of Western Scotland* 1973

National Trust for Scotland *Balmacara, Kintail and the Falls of Glomach*

Nicolson A. *History of Skye* 1995

Ross David *Scottish Place-names* 2001

Stirling A.M.W. *MacDonald of the Isles* 1914

Taylor L.S. *The Quiet Stones*

Watson W.J. *Celtic Place Names of Scotland*

Youngson A.J. *After the Forty-five*

The Skye Games 121st Year 1877–1998

Other Sources:

Census 1851–71

Collin's Encyclopaedia of Scotland

Highlands and Islands Emigration Society

Inverness Advertiser, 24th Feb 1852

Inverness Archives

MacDonald Estate Papers

The Old Statistical Account for Portree 1791

The New Statistical Account for Portree 1841

Parish Records

APPENDIX 1

Chronology of Portree

(Abbreviations: B – Built; ER – Estate Records; List – Listed Building; (S) – Grading of listing)

1493 – Last meeting of the Council of the Lord of the Isles attended by MacNicol of Portray.

1540 – Visit of King James V to (The Harbour of) Portree.

1720–21 – Acc for what was paid out for the Brewery at Portree by J. MacMillan.

1730 – First church built (approx. on site of present Medical Centre) when Portree became a Parish.

1745 – Prince Charlie arrived in Portree. Had dinner in MacNab's Inn before leaving for Raasay.

1750 – Old graveyard opened.

1765 – Plans drawn up by Sir James MacDonald for a new village at Portree. Only built the school before he died in 1766.

1773 – Dr Johnson and Boswell at MacNab's Inn.

1797 – Plans drawn up for Chamberlain's House (Portree House). Mill rebuilt and Inn repaired.

1799 – Old Statistical Account written by Rev Alexander Campbell, schoolmaster. Rev John Nicolson of Scorrybreck, parish minister, died and was succeeded by Alex. Campbell, parochial teacher, from Corlarach, near Dunvegan.

1800 – Built Jail. List B.

1803 – Thomas Telford came to the Highlands.

1804 – ER. Village houses built and mill repaired.

1805 – Mill destroyed by fire.

1806 – ER. Building Chamberlain's House, Portree Mill and Mill lade. Repairs to counting house and joiners shop. Cont. building village houses. Built road from shore to Chamberlain's House. Repair Jail House, Public House at Portree and offices. Continue building village houses.

1807 – Chamberlain's House completed (Portree House). List B.

1809 – ER. Chamberlain's House and Office. Repair School House, Mill and village houses. Whitewashing room occupied by John MacLean, Merchant and Angus MacDonald, Messenger.

1810 – Map: Innkeeper's Land – Homefarm Rd to Staffin Rd. Miller's Land – Staffin Rd to Scorry Burn. Schoolmaster's Land – outwards from Mill dam to Home farm Rd – Inn and two houses further up Bank St. A building across Green from Inn – see old map!

1810 – ER. Building Chamberlain's House (? It was finished 3 years before!) and Offices. Repairing village houses. Continue building village houses. Two engravings of Portree by Daniells showing prison, inn and Chamberlain's House.

1811 – House and office of Chamberlain (repairs?) and garden wall. Cont. building village houses. Village House fitted up for stable to the inn. (Portree Butchers). Repairs to Chamberlain's House.

1814 – Map of plans to drain the Moss – drains to run across moss and trees to be planted beside (present) sale ground.

1816 – School House.

1820 – Church completed (Black Memorial Hall, then Dovetail). List C (S) Manse built for it at Pienmore, Braes Rd.

1823 – Enclosing and planting ground near Portree (where?) Will Henderson, gardener.

1824 – Draining and planting ground in the neighbourhood of Portree. (Again, where?) Dr Alexander MacLeod, Dr Ban, planted the Lump with trees and shrubs and built the tower.

1825 – Drained the loch at Monkstot – Dr Ban again.

1828 – Building additional accommodation to Farmhouse at Scorrybreck.

1829 – Alex MacLeod building sheepfank at farm of Scorrybreck. Intended improvements – Drain and enclose Moss, west of Portree, to build farm. Built new farmhouse at Portree. (Homefarm?) Dr MacLeod suggests encouragement for fishermen round the bay south of the village, and improvement of Moss – building a road through it.

1830 – National Bank – Royal Bank of Scotland.

1830 – Plan of village of Portree, showing design for its extension.

1832–33 – Accounts for Bosville Terr., Old Inn, National Bank (Royal), House at Portree Shore, Wentworth St, Bayfield (not Slignach), School croft, Portree Mill and croft, Shulishadder, Grndoffice and croft, Shulishadder and Lotts, Fisherfield.

1839 – Built Beaumont Crescent. List C (S).

1845 – H. MacDonald granted ground for building house at Viewfield.

1847 – United Presbyterian Church – Free Church.

1848 – Hogg's Woollen Manufactory.

1849–50 – Rents – John Ross. Portree Inn.

1850 – Map of Drains and Water. Stables between Lane and Square (See Records of Estate, 1811 – Village House fitted up stable to the inn) School – pencilled in across the Street (approx the café). Bank (North of Scotland) – King's Haven Hotel, now part of the Bosville. Dougal MacMillan's Feu – SE corner of the square. Jail, in the Square, Wentworth St, Bank St, Bosville Terr, Beaumont Cresc, Shore St (Douglas Row), Cooperage at end of B.C., Inn at Royal Hotel corner, Old Inn, half way up Bank St, New Scorrybreck House.

1850 – Plan of Pier (proposed improvements). The pier then was simply Douglas Row without the houses with a slipway at the end. It was proposed to replace the slip with a proper pier.

1854 – Rents – Viewfield Cottage and Park – Harry MacDonald.

Fancy Hill (the Lump) – Donald MacIntosh

Portree Hill (Stormy Hill).

Heathfield, 10 tenants

Heath Cottage – Miss MacAskill

Victoria Cottage (built by Ewan MacKenzie's grandfather – or great-grandfather) – Miss C. MacAskill

Manufactory – Lawrence Skene (S. Hogg Trustee)

Portree Smithy (or stables) and Free Church stance (Old Mill Showroom, now Bakery) Bayfield Smithy

1855 – United Free Church (Church of Scotland).

1857 – United Free Church Manse (Braedownie). List C(S).

1859 – Union (or Combination) Poorhouse. Archi. Ross & Joass.

1866 – North of Scotland Bank (Clydesdale / Skene's) List B.

1867 – Court House. List B.

1873 – Caledonian Bank (Bank of Scotland). List B.

1875 – Portree Hotel. New Secondary School.

1875–79 – expenditure on pier.

1878 – Skye Gathering Hall.

1881 – John MacKay of Home Farm, Portree and tacksman of Ben Lee unwilling (or could not afford) to renew lease.

1881–82 – Acc. Included sums spent on New Lodge near Portree (Cuillin Hills Hotel) (approx £2000) and new Shooting Lodge at Sconser.

1882 – 'Battle of Braes'. 'Clansman' steamed into Portree Bay at low tide (policemen on board to quell riots!) and ran aground some distance from the pier.

1883 – Episcopalian Church, St Columba's (with tower). List C(S). Replaced one built of corrugated iron.

1890 – Post Office – moved to the Green from Wentworth St. (Full circle?).

1892 – Ross Memorial Hospital (An Tuirieann, now UHI collage).

1893 – Free Presbyterian Church.

1896 – Bayfield House (Parkhouse, now Indian Restaurant).

1900 – Marine Hotel (Oil Depot).

1911 – Road past Storr Lochs to Staffin.

1912 – Masonic Hall (built by the late John Davidson's father) Drill Hall.

1913 – School courtyard roofed in and science block built.

1922 – Poorhouse converted to Margaret Carnagie Hostel for Girls.

1933 – Elgin Hostel for Boys.

1935c – Beaton's Garage moved from pier to Dunvegan Rd. Then Stormont's?

APPENDIX 2

Occupations and Ages 1841[i]

Agricultural Labourers

1. Hector MacLeod 25
2. Angus Nicolson 50
3. Niel Beaton 40
4. Donald Buchanan 15
5. Donald Buchanan 75
6. John Shaw 30
7. George MacLeod 35
8. James MacIntosh 20
9. Gilbert Stuart 70
10. Malcolm MacDougal 35
11. Peter MacKay 25
12. Donald Graham 25
13. Sam Nicolson 25
14. Donald Nicolson 30
15. Angus Macdonald 75
16. Duncan MacIntosh 40
17. Don Buchanan 45
18. Ewan Ferguson 60
19. Dougal Colquhoun 50
20. Alex MacLeod 70
21. Alex MacPherson 60

Bakers

1. Daniel Duncan 35
2. Duncan Frazer 35

Bankers/Clerks/Writers

1. Roderick MacLeod 70
2. Harry MacDonald 35
3. Donald MacKinnon 35
4. Kenneth MacKinnon 75
5. Kenneth MacAskill 35
6. Laurence Skene 25
7. Charles Shaw 25
8. James Frazer 25
9. Lewis Jamieson 30

Boat Builder

1. Archie Colquhoun 30

Civil Servants

1. John Paterson 35
2. William MacIntosh 40
3. John Man[?] 45

[i] From the 1841 census.

Clergyman

1. Charles Miller 30

Coopers

1. Donald Frazer 30
2. John Buchanan 50

Fishermen

1. Armiger Nicolson 30
2. John MacDougal 55
3. James MacIntosh 25

Gardeners

1. Donald MacDonald 40
2. John MacPherson 45

Handloom weavers

1. Duncan MacCallum 65
2. Mary MacDonald 30
3. Catherine MacQueen 25

Hawker/Tinkers

1. John Collins 60
2. Thomas Prin/dgle[?] 25
3. Donald Matheson 65
4. Betty Lyon 70
5. Flora Gibson 50
6. William MacIver 35

House Carpenters

1. Angus Nicolson
2. Lauchlan MacKinnon 45
3. William Proudfoot 25
4. John Beaton 40

Independent

1. Ann MacAskill 30
2. Mary MacAskill 35
3. Christy MacAskill 50
4. Mary MacLeod 30
5. Margaret Nicolson 50
6. C,M,A, MacLeod 30,35,40
7. Lewis Necker 55
8. Mary Matheson 40
9. Mary Miller 25
10. Christy MacLeod 20
11. John MacLean 60
12. Rachel Kelly 40
13. Marjory Kelly 20
14. Isabella Nicolson 50
15. Catherine MacLachlin 30
16. Ann Robertson 65

Innkeepers

1. John Jamieson 60
2. Hugh Cameron 35

Mantua maker/Dressmakers

1. Flora McNeil 35
2. Flora MacQueen 40
3. William & Grace Harris 25
4. Christy King(?) 20
5. Effy MacInnes 50
6. Flora MacLean 30
7. Ann Matheson 30

Mariner/Sailors

1. Nathanial MacNiel 35
2. John MacKenzie 25
3. Niel MacDonald 30

4. William Stewart 30
5. Alex Nicolson 30
6. Peter Beaton 20
7. Norman Campbell 25
8. Kenneth MacRae 35

Masons

1. John Ross 35
2. Alex MacKinnon 50
3. Angus Morrison 35
4. Malcolm Macintyre 30
5. Alex MacLeod 20
6. John Nicolson 50

Merchants/Shopkeepers

1. William Cumming 30
2. Alex MacNaughton 30
3. William MacIntyre 30
4. John Cameron 40
5. Malcolm Bruce 50
6. Donald MacDonald 25
7. John Morrison 25
8. Donald MacDonald 30
9. John Beaton 35
10. Norman Nicolson 35
11. Charles MacLeod 30

Midwives

1. Ann MacQueen 65
2. Mary Matheson 75

Miller

1. Donald MacLeod 45

Paupers

1. Mary MacFarlane 90
2. Marion Martin 25
3. Betty Shaw 45
4. Ann Buchanan 35
5. Marion MacDonald 40
6. Ann Nicolson 75
7. Betty Nicolson 70
8. Rachel MacPherson 40
9. Rachel Beaton 35
10. Rachel Matheson 80
11. Ann MacDonald 70
12. Catherine MacDonald 65
13. John MacRae 80

Postie

1. Alex MacDonald 25
2. Duncan MacDonald 45
3. Angus Kelly 35

Saddler

1. Alex MacLean 30

Schoolmaster

1. Murdo MacDonald 40

Shoemakers

1. Roderick MacDonald 40
2. Ewan Kennedy 35
3. Donald MacCrimmon 25
4. John MacDonald 20
5. Finlay MacRae 25
6. Allan MacSween 40
7. John Chisholm 30

Shoemakers (cont'd)

8. Archie Munro 55
9. Ewan MacDonald 35

Smiths

1. Donald Cameron 40
2. John MacDonald 15

Tailors

1. Martin MacInnes 30
2. John MacFadyen 35
3. Finlay MacDonald 21
4. Peter Nicolson 50
5. Hector MacLean 60
6. William Ferguson 30

Watchmaker

1. David Simpson 35

THE ISLANDS BOOK TRUST –
high quality books on island themes in English and Gaelic

Based in Lewis, the Islands Book Trust are a charity committed to furthering understanding and appreciation of the history of Scottish islands in their wider Celtic and Nordic context. We do this through publishing books, organising talks and conferences, visits, radio broadcasts, research and education on island themes. For details of membership of the Book Trust, which will keep you in touch with all our publications and other activities, see *www.theislandsbooktrust.com*, phone 01851 830316, or visit Laxay at the address below where a good selection of our books is available to buy.

The Islands Book Trust, Laxay Hall, Laxay, Isle of Lewis,
HS2 9PJ. Tel: 01851 830316